epta UK

Teachers' choice 1
Piano collection

Favourite pieces selected by teachers

Compiled and edited by Mark Tanner

FABER *ff* MUSIC

In memory of Carola Grindea (1914–2009)
Romanian-born British pianist who established
the European Piano Teachers Association in 1978

'This special collection of piano music contains an enormous range of expression and style. It includes some of the most famous and universally popular piano pieces in the repertoire, selected by piano teachers from all over the UK who are members of EPTA (European Piano Teachers Association). Though the selection is highly varied, it has all stood the test of time and proved to be inspirational and rewarding in piano lessons. The broadly graded format provides aspiring players with a structure and framework for progression, hence the music should appeal not only to the players themselves, but also to their families and friends – the people who hear them practising and playing regularly. Enjoy this wide spectrum of styles and perspectives!'

Murray McLachlan, Chair, EPTA UK

'EPTA was founded in 1978 by Carola Grindea, who was so impressed by the success of ESTA (European String Teachers Association) that she wanted to give pianists and piano teachers similar opportunities. It was her intention to unite pianists all over the world to meet together and exchange views on pedagogy and pianism. Forty years on EPTA is thriving, with associations throughout Europe and affiliated associations worldwide: USA, Israel, India, China, Argentina and South America. The standard of piano teaching is rapidly escalating all the time, and piano pedagogy is now an integral part of study in all British Conservatoires. It is wonderful to have this publication ready to celebrate forty years of EPTA, and it is hoped that all teachers and students will benefit from this wealth of repertoire as they work through a diversity of enormously rewarding pieces.'

Nadia Lasserson, Organising Secretary, EPTA Europe

Acknowledgements go to Lesley Rutherford and Emily Bevington for their careful editing and invaluable creative input. Thanks also to the EPTA Management Committee, in particular to Nadia Lasserson, Murray McLachlan and Karen Marshall. Additional proof-reading kindly undertaken by Gily Poznansky.

© 2019 by Faber Music Ltd
This edition first published in 2019
Bloomsbury House, 74–77 Great Russell Street, London WC1B 3DA
Music processed by Sarah Lofthouse
Cover design by Susan Clarke
Printed in England by Caligraving Ltd
All rights reserved

ISBN10: 0-571-54125-9
EAN13: 978-0-571-54125-6

To buy Faber Music publications or to find out about the full range of titles available please contact your local music retailer or Faber Music sales enquiries:
Faber Music Ltd, Burnt Mill, Elizabeth Way, Harlow CM20 2HX
Tel: +44 (0) 1279 82 89 82   Fax: +44 (0) 1279 82 89 83
sales@fabermusic.com   fabermusicstore.com

Contents

Introduction 4

African Dawn Armstrong 5

Rocking Gurlitt 6

Minuet in F Mozart 7

Tempo di minuetto Hook 8

The Wood Fairies Carroll 9

The Wonderful Wizard Wedgwood 10

Lesson in C Diabelli 11

Scherzo – Duet Diabelli 12

Musette in D J S Bach 14

Skedaddle Milne 15

Children at Play Bartók 16

Now is the Month of Maying Morley arr. Gritton 17

Deutsche Tänze Haydn 18

Bärentanz Schumann 19

Dragon Dance McLeod 20

Zur Sonnenuntergangsstunde Schmitz 21

Minuet in G Petzold 22

Sonatina in C major Clementi 24

Dance of the Sugar Plum Fairy Tchaikovsky arr. Gritton 26

Philippa's Jig Murray McLeod 27

Chocolate Car Park Wedgwood 30

Sonatina in F major Beethoven 32

Innocence Burgmüller 34

Solfeggio in D J C F Bach 35

All White on the Night Kember 36

Fröhlicher Landmann Schumann 37

Sonatina in C major Kuhlau 38

Upon Reflection Hammond 41

Ballade Burgmüller 42

Prelude in C minor J S Bach 44

Indian Pony Race Glover 46

Introduction

It has been a treat to reacquaint myself with a treasure-trove of piano music in putting together these two books. In its 40th anniversary year, EPTA UK wanted to honour its membership by asking them to nominate their personal favourite pieces and also to cherry-pick from a range of standard repertoire. The hope and ambition for these two bumper volumes is to appeal to an audience of pianists and teachers alike, both within and outside the EPTA community.

In addition, I have added a handful of my own 'Editor's Choices': pieces by James Hook, Thomas Morely and Heather Hammond, a delightful new piece, *Dragon Dance*, by John McLeod, and the foot-tapping *Philippa's Jig* by Margaret Murray McLeod. For the most part this has been to strengthen the contribution made by female composers, or perhaps to bolster certain styles not otherwise voted for at a particular grade. You may stumble across music entirely new to you, such as the exquisite *The Chimes* by William Baines, a prolific English composer from the turn of the 20th century who tragically died at the tender age of 23. No composer in Book 2 (grades 5–8) has been included more than once – not even Bach, Mozart or Chopin – in an attempt to achieve as wide a representation as possible. There is a conspicuous dearth of Classical sonata movements here, simply to avoid soaking up too many pages.

A thought or two about the grading. Anyone who plays or teaches the piano will be aware that beyond the most obvious 'machinery', duration and surface detail of any given piece, it's actually rather difficult to assign a specific grade. For one thing, exam boards may alter their position over the years. For another thing, the speed at which a piece ultimately goes and the quality of detail a player is able to include in their performance will both impact significantly on its proposed difficulty. In the end, it's the performance that's of a certain standard, of course, not the piece itself; grading is merely a convenient, blunt-edged tool for categorising music. Hence in both books, the pieces have been presented progressively in standard as far as possible, while still enabling good page turns. Where relevant there is a numbered icon referencing the Edexcel GCSE Music performance difficulty level, for a further steer on repertoire standard. Up to **3** indicates less difficult repertoire, the standard level of difficulty for GCSE is **4** , and **5** is more difficult.

You will, I am sure, enjoy reading the comments from EPTA members; these are often coupled with performance advice which you can savour or pass over as you see fit. This is repertoire that has been loved and taught worldwide, and we pianists are fortunate to have had an abundance of composers who've honoured the early learner, from Bach and Burgmüller to Bartók. Whether you turn these pages in your capacity as a piano teacher or as a lifelong student of the instrument, on EPTA's behalf I warmly invite you to share and profit from this enduring bounty of music.

Mark Tanner

African Dawn

'A brilliant introduction to the wonderful sonority of the piano, making adventurous use of pedal. The atmosphere of an African dawn is captured through simple yet highly effective use of fifths and a syncopated rhythm. The possibility of learning this by rote if desired makes it ideal for a young learner. I particularly enjoy the use of different registers, encouraging freedom of movement, whilst through musical imagery the pupil can learn to play expressively.' Alison Mathews, Surrey

June Armstrong

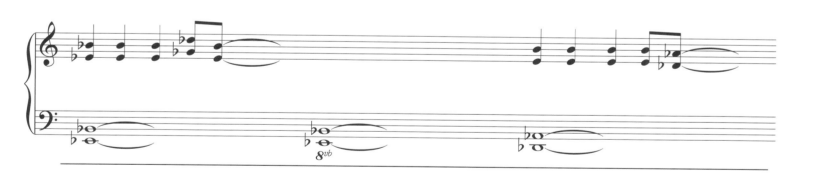

Rocking Op.117, No.6

'This piece is ideal for sparking a fledgling pianist's imagination. There is opportunity for story-telling with the feeling of rocking created by the lilting rhythm of the music. Packed with useful teaching material, *Rocking* contains many comfortable chord shapes, while its time signature calls for an effective balance of melody and accompaniment.' Rowan Cozens, Newark

Cornelius Gurlitt

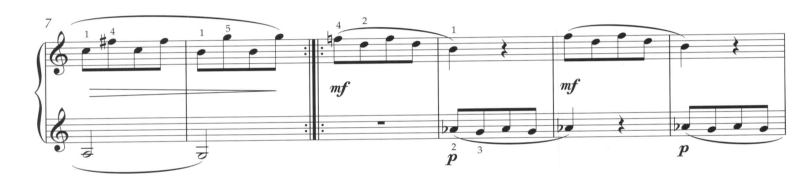

Minuet in F K.2

'A beautifully balanced piece, both in its form and in the right hand's repeated phrasing.
A useful piece for investigating keys, modulations and structure. The diminuendos at the
end of each phrase are an ideal way to teach cadences. The dynamics and slurs are also
important, and the piece contains many worthwhile teaching points.' Belinda Swift, Leeds

Wolfgang Amadeus Mozart

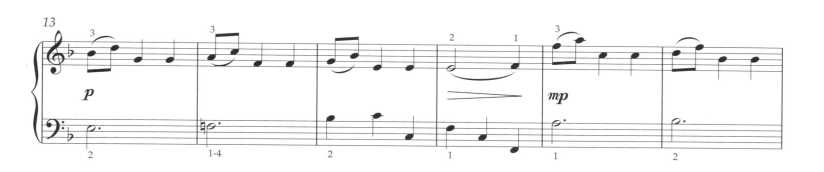

Tempo di minuetto Op.37, No.2

'This is a perfect first concert item for an elementary student. All in one hand position, the student gets a workout in phrasing, varied articulation, contrasting dynamics and even an occasional triplet thrown in for good measure. Uncomplicated and accessible, yet impressive to listen to, this is a welcome addition for teachers who want to boost a young pianist's confidence.' Mark Tanner, Editor

James Hook

The Wood Fairies

'This is such a cleverly written piece. My students are particularly drawn to its dance-like character, and many have had fun performing it. There is plenty of technical detail for the level, including the need for wrist flexibility and a good contrast between legato and staccato playing.' Marcel Zidani, Evesham

Walter Carroll

The Wonderful Wizard

'A real toe-tapper of a piece; the left-hand's steady beat helps to give the right hand a confident swing rhythm. Children love this piece, and it's a great way to practise the technical challenges of playing legato against staccato, as well as balancing chords against a melody.' Hilary Garrett, West Yorkshire

Pam Wedgwood

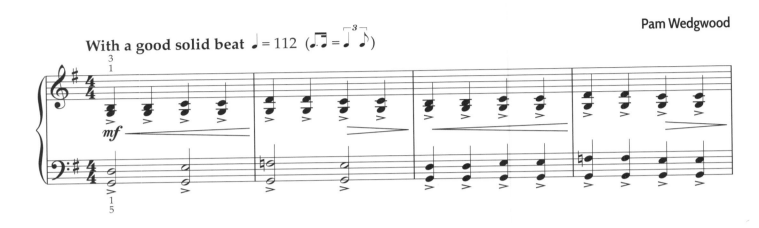

Lesson in C

'There's nothing too complicated about this lovely miniature. Adults as well as children love it.
Packed with enjoyable musical ingredients and different chords in block and broken positions,
your students will gain a real sense of achievement playing it.' Sheila Wright, The Wolds

Anton Diabelli

Duet: Secondo

Scherzo

'I've used this *Scherzo* for years – students like it as it sounds impressive. Including a variety of articulation, dynamics and a tempo change, this playful duet develops lots of important skills. On top of that, it's a thoroughly enjoyable piece, so I use it regularly at my pupils' concerts. All in all, it's easy to play and always a winner.' Janet Lawrence, Selby

Anton Diabelli

Duet: Primo

Scherzo

Anton Diabelli

Musette in D BWV Anh.126

'This *Musette* is one of the memorable highlights from the Anna Magdalena Notebook. It really isn't a million miles away from contemporary dance or rock music, with its driving rhythm, simple harmony and catchy hook. It allows players to develop precision when navigating the keyboard, together with dynamic control.' Andrew Eales, Milton Keynes

Johann Sebastian Bach

Skedaddle from *Little Peppers*

'Fun to play and a good introduction to syncopation, swung quavers, dynamic and articulation contrasts. Children really enjoy getting to grips with its walking bass, and there is so much more for them to explore as they learn the piece.' Ann Burden, Peterborough

Elissa Milne

Children at Play from *For Children*, No.1

'This piece is all about independence of the hands, being able to play legato in one hand and slurs in the other – and then swap around in an instant. A fun way to introduce the piece is to get your pupil to rub their tummy and pat their head at the same time!' Hilary Garrett, West Yorkshire

Béla Bartók

Now is the Month of Maying

'This infectious tune, complete with boisterous 'fa-la-la' refrain, was originally conceived as a 'ballett' for five voices. The challenge in this first-rate arrangement is to bring all the counterpoint to life at a spirited two-in-a-bar. The left hand claims our attention in a number of unexpected places, hence all the little details warrant the utmost care. Crystal clear finger work, together with pristine rhythms, will ensure a charismatic performance.' Mark Tanner, Editor

Thomas Morley
Arr. Peter Gritton

Deutsche Tänze German Dances

'Haydn's music is always packed with humour and charm. This beautiful pair of German dances
require careful finger work and a light touch. Challenges for the young pianist include voicing,
requiring careful balancing of the hands, though the music's demands bring lots of rewards.
There is much fun and satisfaction to be gained from the articulation and ornaments – ideal
preparation for Classical sonatinas. Make the most of the *fz* markings and aim to shape
phrases with elegance – your audience will appreciate it!'   Kathryn Page, Cheshire

Joseph Haydn

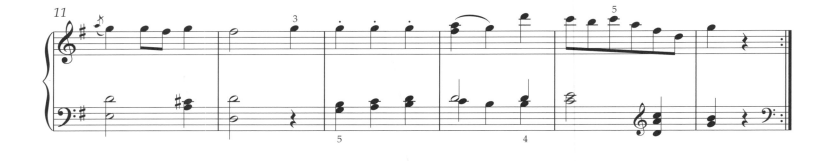

Bärentanz   Bear's Dance

'Younger students love this piece. The bass ostinato can be used to improvise over, and there are important skills waiting to be developed, such as performing accented fifths and playing acciaccaturas with flair! Expressive playing is encouraged through the imagery of a bear dancing, and this is a valuable piece of early repertoire for inspiring use of the pedal. With several repeated sections, this piece should be quick to learn.' Karen Marshall, York

Robert Schumann

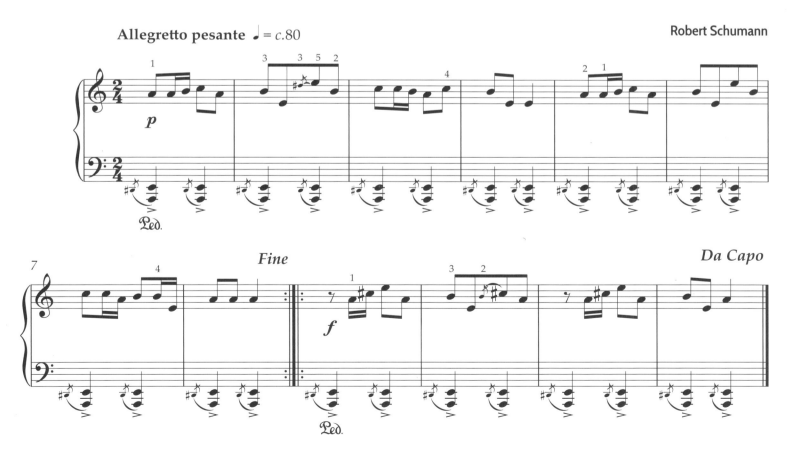

Dragon Dance

'There is much daring pianism waiting to be threaded into your performance of this piece. Launch yourself fearlessly at this bitonal, fire-breathing dance (it all fits beautifully under the fingers) – there's nothing faintly polite about all those cluster chords. Among its challenges are sustaining rhythmic energy, legato against staccato, and of course a highly combustible finale.' Mark Tanner, Editor

John McLeod

Hold L.H. chord until sounds die away.

Zur Sonnenuntergangsstunde At Sunset

'This piece is a delight to teach, with opportunities to develop rubato, pedal control and melody-sharing between the hands. Clef and time signature changes – along with hand-crossing – also add to the challenge. This is a real winner with my students and regularly pops up in our studio recitals.' Liz Giannopoulos, London

Manfred Schmitz

Minuet in G

'This piece is a great introduction to contrapuntal playing and independence of the hands.
At the same time, it will encourage pupils to feel the dance movement built into the phrases.
The music demands great focus from young players to control the specific touch in each
hand while maintaining the music's rhythmic sweep, which will in turn coax out its natural
elegance.' Nadia Lasserson, London

Attrib. Christian Petzold

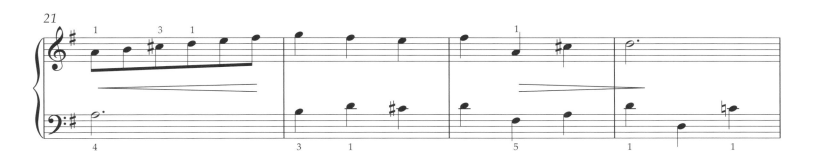

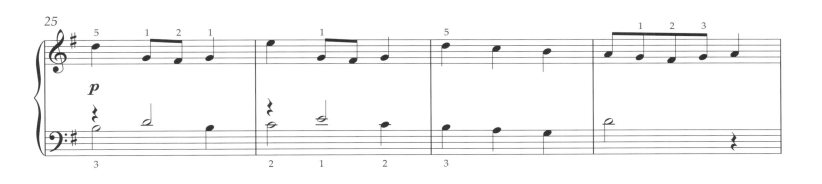

Sonatina in C major Op.36, No.1

'I enjoy teaching this piece because it's so bright and playful. A great introduction to the Classical style, covering patterns and articulation which students will find in lots of repertoire of the period. It's excellent for showing the importance of scales and arpeggios (not to mention practising with the correct fingering). Teachers can use the piece to introduce modulation to the dominant, basic chord progressions and phrasing. It's also ideal for teaching how musical elements such as dynamics and texture contribute to sonata form.' Ana Fontecha, York

Muzio Clementi

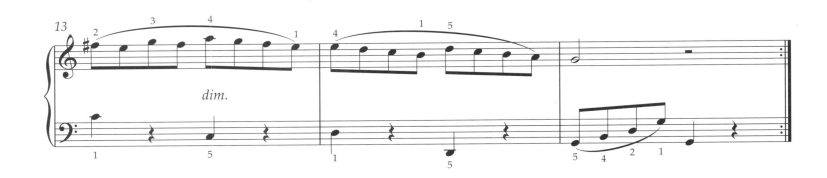

Dance of the Sugar Plum Fairy

'This is a beautiful, cheeky piece by Tchaikovsky. An excellent vehicle for practising
a light staccato in the left hand. The right hand's challenge is to play off the beat in $\frac{2}{4}$.
It's also a great piece to help players develop a wide dynamic range, from **pp** to **f**.'
Matthew Palmer, Doncaster

Pyotr Ilyich Tchaikovsky
Arr. Peter Gritton

Philippa's Jig

'I'm confident this jovial jig will be a real winner with teachers and pupils alike. It's great fun to play, with hand-crossing galore and a banquet of carefully judged markings to feast on. An occasional explosion of dynamics or other unexpected diversion adds to its rustic appeal, and yet ballet shoes might be more suitable than clogs for this brisk dance. Find a speed which allows you to play crisply and vigorously, but tidily, too.' Mark Tanner, Editor

Margaret Murray McLeod

poco rit.　　　　meno mosso

rall. poco a poco　　　　Tempo primo

Chocolate Car Park

'I've always loved Pam Wedgwood's music. She was one of the first composers to make 'jazzy' music accessible to young pianists. *Chocolate Car Park* includes plenty of technical challenges, whilst also being an exciting performance piece.' Heather Hammond, York

Pam Wedgwood

Sonatina in F major (1st movement)

'This has long been a favourite for younger players to tackle; it has immediacy and is memorably dramatic. Whether it was actually composed by Beethoven is debatable, yet its sweeping scalic runs, daring modulations and challenging shifts in harmonic rhythm are musically rewarding as well as educationally beneficial. This is a terrific choice for building confidence and flair in a young player.' Murray McLachlan, Manchester

Attrib. Ludwig van Beethoven

Innocence Op.100, No.5

'One of my go-to pieces, it's written in F major, brimming with scales and packed with delightful articulation. The title can trigger useful discussion in lessons, and the deeper you look, the more there is to reward a diligent approach.' Sue Craxton, Dorset

Johann Friedrich Burgmüller

Solfeggio in D

'A fantastic introduction to the Bach family for the early-intermediate level player! A rippling effect is created through the balance between the hands. The player will need to keep a consistent rhythmic flow in the broken chord semiquavers. This will provide opportunities to study sequences and chord progressions, and how these affect the mood of a piece. Pupils can identify different colours within the harmony and add their own dynamics in keeping with the rising and falling phrases.' Amy Wakefield, Congleton

Johann Christoph Friedrich Bach

All White on the Night

'This has always been a favourite with my students. Though uncomplicated, it is packed with valuable teaching content from chord voicing and syncopation to articulation. The phrasing calls for careful finger work to keep the quavers even within the musical shapes. Using pentatonics, chromatics, colourful chords and a bold range of dynamics, this piece is fun for performer and listener alike!' Karen Marshall, York

John Kember

Reproduced from *Jazz Piano Studies 1* (Faber Music).

Fröhlicher Landmann Happy Farmer Op.68, No.2

'A children's classic. The catchy tune will appeal to all students, but they will have to pay close attention to the fingering so that they can negotiate awkward intervals in the left hand. This piece is good for practising melody and accompaniment all in one hand.'
Hilary Garrett, West Yorkshire

Robert Schumann

Fresh and lively (Vigoroso e allegramente)

Sonatina in C major Op.55, No.3

'The bright, lively character of this sonatina makes it an appealing introduction to Classical style. It does not begin loudly, however; the dolce marking suggests a gentler, more persuasive tone. Contrasts between *f* and *p* abound, but phrasing will need a natural rise and fall to add shape. Almost all quavers should be played staccato; just a few (such as in bars 9 and 11) sound better legato, as does the second beat, quaver-two semiquavers figure (bar 13 and similar). Wrist staccato is needed for the quavers in sixths and fifths, with care to balance melody and accompaniment.' Margaret Murray McLeod, Edinburgh

Friedrich Kuhlau

Upon Reflection

'What a delightful way to become adept at pedalling. Used too little, the music will sound dry and static, and yet used excessively it will disintegrate into a featureless soup. The syncopated rhythms are what keeps the piece moving forward with enough energy to keep its reflective message afloat. The mood is not always tranquil – be courageous with the grander music and savour the left hand's chance at the tune later on.' Mark Tanner, Editor

Heather Hammond

Reproduced from *The Intermediate Pianist – Book 2* (ed. Karen Marshall & Heather Hammond), Faber Music.

Ballade Op.100, No.15

'I use this piece to stir children's imagination, and they easily home in on the dramatic effect.
The contrasts built into the piece are fantastic, and there is a huge amount of vivid detail to
pull out in lessons and when at home practising. The music's rhythmic drive is paramount,
and this also makes for some challenges of hand coordination, balance and sense of overall
musical direction.' Gwen Nathan, Kent

Johann Friedrich Burgmüller

Prelude in C minor BWV 847

'This dramatic piece is inspirational and yet approachable for pianists of all ages. Its figurations encourage the development of focused finger facility as well as harmonic awareness. Try playing each bar as a block chord in order to grasp how smoothly and ingeniously Bach moves through each progression. The piece is also excellent for developing an economy of movement and logical fingering.' Murray McLachlan, Manchester

Johann Sebastian Bach

Indian Pony Race

'And they're off! This is a gallop from the outset, but allow a measured pace; control is needed to arrive safely at the finish line, and rhythm is especially key here, particularly the definition of the semiquaver figurations and the final scramble for the line. Off-beats need to be precisely placed and a loose wrist will aid both the staccato and timing. Don't neglect the expressive features either; achieving the final quaver accents in a bar takes skill, and the hairpins in the middle section are full of narrative. Much of the piece lies comfortably under the fingers, but paradoxically it also covers a significant amount of piano geography – a good example of a piece best played from memory.' Meurig Thomas, Bath

David Carr Glover

EPTA's Piano Professional series

The Foundations of Technique is about putting into practise everything that you wish to do at the instrument. This new and innovative approach to technique is for everyone interested in improving their piano playing and teaching.

Piano Technique in Practice is for all pianists and piano teachers. Following on from the widely acclaimed *The Foundations of Technique*, this informative text offers a more detailed guide to piano playing for pianists at every level.

The Psychology of Piano Technique is much more than a musical self-help book, dealing with a large range of topics and problems which pianists of all levels constantly face.

The Mindful Pianist presents amateurs and professionals with a fresh perspective on playing and performing. Applying the concept of mindfulness to the piano, this invaluable text explores the crucial connection between mind and body: how an alert, focused mind fosters playing that is more compelling, more refined and ultimately more rewarding.

If you are a piano teacher, why not think about joining EPTA?

EPTA – the European Piano Teachers Association, UK – was founded in 1978 by Carola Grindea. The aims of EPTA UK are to promote excellence in piano teaching and performance, to bring teachers and performers together and to raise standards within the profession. All members receive public liability insurance and a number of other benefits.

- The Association undertakes to exchange ideas, learn from others, share the experience of high-quality performances and masterclasses, undertake research, and to share information through meetings, seminars, courses, conferences and publications. Regional networks of teachers, supported by the work of Regional Organisers, help to bring these objectives together.

- New initiatives are coming on stream all the time, recent among these being EPTA Education, which as well as offering a teacher mentoring scheme, has developed a growing number of exciting collaborations in delivering residential and single-day CPD events around the UK.

- EPTA's flagship magazine, *Piano Professional* (free to all members), alongside a growing number of books directed at furthering high-quality piano playing and teaching, continue to increase the literature in valuable ways. Members' pupils are eligible to apply for bursaries towards tuition in cases of hardship, indeed the encouragement of piano playing, at all ages and abilities, is central to EPTA's philosophy.

If you would like to apply to become a member of EPTA UK, either at Professional, Associate or Student level, please contact the Administrator at admin@epta-uk.org.

Faber Music Ltd, Burnt Mill, Elizabeth Way, Harlow CM20 2HX
Tel: +44 (0) 1279 828982   Fax: +44 (0) 1279 828983
sales@fabermusic.com   fabermusicstore.com